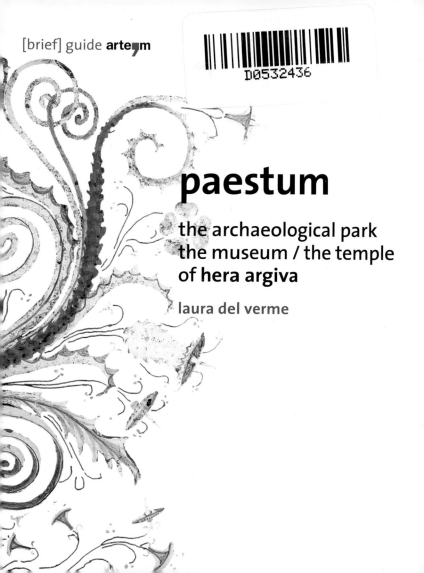

paestum

the archaeological park
the museum / the temple
of hera argiva

laura del verme

table of contents

[summary]

Discover the temple of **Hera**, at the mouth of the river Sele where the Greek colonists landed, and marvel at the temples of **Paestum**, the best-preserved archaeological site in the entire Greek world in the Mediterranean, "the most perfectly intact temple [of Neptune] of all Greek architecture" [A. Maiuri].

Visit the archaeological museum to see the vestiges of Sybarites, Enotrians, Campanians, Lucanians and Romans, the monument to eternity that is the **Tomb of the Diver**, the evidence of Italic civilisation, neolithic cemeteries and Lucanian tombs.

Ancient Poseidonia (Paestum) has an aura of eternity that cannot be erased by time and deserves more than a fleeting visit. It is only two hours' drive from the Bay of Naples, just over an hour from Potenza and about three hours from Bari. It lies at at the centre of the colourful historical and natural heritage of the province of Salerno [Pontecagnano, Agropoli, Eboli, Alento, intact medieval hill towns, Padula, Castelcivita, Pertosa, Morigerati].

By popular acclaim, Paestum is generally considered to be the 'capital' of the **Cilento**, **Vallo di Diano** and **Alburni National Park**. It is the emblem of the rich environmental, historical and cultural heritage which is largely unknown to 'global tourism' and, alarmingly often, to local inhabitants who are unaware of their own sedimented identity. However, this identity can provide the basis for new prospects for a sustainable economy and a 'high quality of life' if only it is able to take advantage of its **material culture, agriculture** [olives, wines, artichokes, buffalos], healthy **diet** and **cultural heritage** which we must endeavour to safeguard and renew. Page after page, from the blue of the **archaeological park**, to the **red** of the **museum collections**, and to the area of the **Temple of Hera at Foca Sele**, each topic has its own **map**, **numerical references** to **sites** and to **key images**. This **[brief] guide** is an open invitation to experience the **excitement** of a journey through a boundless history, to explore the area's roots to deserve, without preconceived ideas and fussiness, the life that we want.

the archaeological area of paestum

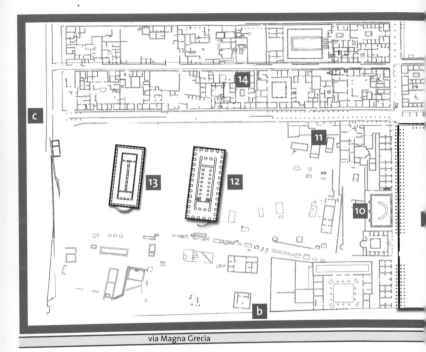

via Magna Grecia

a entrance porta cerere
   (gate of ceres)

b entrance / exit
   main gate

c entrance porta giustizia
   (justice gate)

1 temple of athena
   known as temple of ceres
2 ekklesiasterion
3 heroon
4 pool
5 temple of peace
6 comitium
7 amphitheatre

8 aerarium
9 forum
10 curia
11 thermal baths
12 temple of neptune
13 temple of hera
   known as the basilica
14 residential districts

via Magna Grecia

d national archaeological
museum

ticket office, bookshop
[see pp. 54-55]

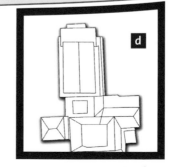

historical background

Paestum is famous worldwide for its striking Greek temples which continue to capture the imagination of visitors. The temples are still intact – few other ancient monuments are so well-preserved – after more than 2,500 years of natural disasters and social upheavals. Paestum regained the position it deserved in European and Mediterranean culture in the mid-eighteenth century as a popular destination of the *Grand Tour* – the journey of exploration and learning that formed the basis, and the elite origins, of modern cultural tourism. In pre-history, the area is associated with the name of the rural district of Gaudo which has brought to light the traces of an imposing cemetery,

the subject of a recent exhibition in the Archaeological Museum. According to Strabo – the father of western geography – the Greek city was founded by Achaean colonists fleeing from Sybaris. The religious area of Agropoli on which the medieval castle stands probably corresponds to the temple of *Poseidon* (Neptune) *Enipeus*, the river god of Thessaly celebrated by the poet Lycophron.

The settlement of *Poseidonia* is bounded to the south by Capodifiume, and contains a mixture of sacred and secular spaces in accordance with the typical urban layout of Greek civilization.

Situated on the boundary with the Etruscan-Campanian world, this defensive outpost of Magna Graecia in the Sele river plain was founded by a small group of Achaean colonists from Sybaris in about 600 BC. Evidence for this is provided by the foundation inscriptions of a small temple (shrine) lying to the south of the temple of *Athena* (known as the temple of Ceres), whose traces are imprinted in the roof of painted ter-

Silver **coin** from Poseidonia 410 BC

The **Temple of Neptune** and the **Basilica** 1933 Samaritani Archive

racotta. The city occupies the limestone shelf in the centre of a large plain stretching from the hills of Capaccio, to the east and the Tyrrhenian Sea to the west.

During the same period, the colonists dedicated a large temple to the goddess *Hera* to the north along the river Sele. Known as the *Heraion*, the temple is situated at the mouth of the Sele, which tradition associates with the deeds of Jason, the hero of the Golden Fleece (the fleece of the golden ram with magic healing powers). Rediscovered in the 1930s by Umberto Zanotti Bianco and Paola Zancani Montuoro, the temple was decorated with carved metopes (now on display in the Archaeological Museum of Paestum), one of the most important religious frieze cycles in the archaic Greek world.

An important further development of the city took place between the mid 6th century BC, with paved streets, new houses, sewers and drainage systems which mark out the urban area.

The area on the northern edge of the settlement was dedicated to *Athena*, while the area to the south was dedicated to *Hera*; both are dominated by the large temples. The rediscovery of the religious buildings in the eighteenth century led to new attempts at interpretation, and the analysis of scholars of the period produced the first 'evocative' names. The **temple of Athena** (late 6th century BC; restored and modified in around 520-510 BC) was identified as the **temple of Ceres**, perhaps due to the suggestion of Vitruvius. In his work *De Architectura* (first century BC), Vitruvius refers to the Greek colonists' custom of building a propitiatory temple at the gates of the city, dedicated to the goddess of harvests and agriculture. Modern archaeological excavations have finally re-established the historical 'truth' thanks to the discovery of votive material and statuettes of the goddess Athena.

The **temple of Hera** (530 BC), the oldest temple in the site, was referred to as a **Basilica** in the eighteenth century: ex votos and inscriptions once again enable the temple to be rightfully restored to its actual association with the wife of Zeus, the queen of the Greek pantheon. Situated in the plain between the two temples, the **agora** (later the Roman forum) was the centre of city life and took on a monumental appearance in this period with the **heroon**, the underground *sacrarium* which the Greeks dedicated to the founder of the city who was worshipped after death as a divine hero. Bronze vases (now in the Archaeological Museum of Paestum) were found in the building. They were still full of honey when excavated and are masterpieces of metal-working in Magna Graecia.

All around there were private houses, with large uninhabited areas. Along the river Sele, there was another cult building dedicated to Hera of which the metopes with dancing girls still survive.

The phase of expansion came to an end in around 480-470 BC with two imposing monuments: the temple known in the eighteenth century as the **temple of Neptune** (mid 5th century BC), the emblem of Doric architecture in the west, was actually dedicated to the cult of Hera or – more likely – to Zeus, as is shown by the painted terracotta statuette with a beard and a bronze crown; the **ekklesiasterion** (480-470 BC) was built in the agora, the area used for public meetings; circular in shape and with tiered seating, the building is a successful combination of taste in terms of its architecture and town planning (later covered with earth and stones by the Romans who, during the republican period, built a shrine in the area with a portico, fountain and storeroom).

The morphology of the cemeteries confirms the conquest of Poseidonia in the last two decades of the fifth century – described by Strabo – by the armies of the Lucanians, an Italic people of Samnite origin. The enormous wealth of the grave goods reveal a new social model: weapons and sophisticated jewellery, reflecting the story of everyday life whose customs and rituals were far removed from the sobriety of Greek Poseidonia: banqueting, imaginary animals, demons and still lifes. In short, aristocratic civilization was immortalised by the painted tombs which today represent, together with the monumental temples, the emblem and destiny of the magical plain of Paestum.

Large-scale urban architectural building was only resumed in the mid-fourth century with the imposing city walls (originally over seven metres high) which are still very impressive today with three kilometres of perimeter wall lining the environmental and historical breadth of the ancient city. There are four main gates: **Porta Aurea** to the north, **Porta della Sirena** to the west, **Porta Giustizia** to the south and **Porta Marina** to the east. The comparison and contrasts between the two identities incorporated within the city's foundation – the Greek spirit and the Italic culture grafted onto it – are transformed, as in all the most fascinating experiences of history, into an inextricable cultural osmosis: a *stele* found in the meeting room, wedged in between two steps, bears an inscription in Oscan, "for received grace", built by the Lucanian magistrate Statis and dedicated to "Iuppiter" (Jupiter); in spite of political and institutional variations, it reflects the continuity in cult practice and civic traditions in about 300 BC.

The threat posed by Rome loomed on the horizon. Poseidonia was asked to take sides in the first Samnite wars, first alongside the army of Pyrrhus and then with the militias of Tarentum. The city, and the Lucanians, were eventually defeated and were forced to accept the status of colony (273 BC). From this moment onwards, Paestum would remain a faithful ally of Rome, even during the Punic wars, and its urban layout underwent radical transformations. During the second century BC, the **temple** known as the '**Tempio della Pace**', with its Corinthian Doric architecture (2nd-1st century BC), was built in the northern side of the forum; dedicated to *Mens Bona* (the Roman deity of reason, called upon to supervise the capacity for discernment of the political class, subsequently became a symbol of the gratitude of freedmen towards the *bona mens* – 'good mind' – of their former masters). The temple splits the **comitium**, or meeting room, in two. During the mid-first century AD, the **amphitheatre** (first century AD; extended between the end of the first and the beginning of the second century AD) was built in the area behind the forum to the north-east. Unfortunately, in 1829, the amphitheatre was cut through the middle by the modern road which runs through the city.

During the Christian era, Paestum maintained and renewed its prestige. In its new guise as a bishop's see, the heart of social life was transferred to the hill of Capaccio Vecchio. *Caput Aquis* was

6 Tomb 21 Andriuolo
detail
central tree and birds
fourth century BC

destroyed in 1246 by Frederick II and fell into the obscurity of memory and 'romantic' ruins. The city was gradually submerged within the mists of the un-

ealthy marsh which was only reclaimed
nder the fascist regime, during the re-
ival of classicism which marked the pre-
ude to the Second World War.

on pages 16 and 17
Giovan Battista Lusieri
**The Temple of Neptune
at Paestum**
private collection

the rose of paestum

It is the symbol of spring and owes its name to the nymph Roda, daughter of Poseidon and Aphrodite. The ancient Greeks referred to it as *rodon*, while the Romans called it *rosa*. Among all the flowers, it is the most treasured and was highly prized in antiquity due to its beauty, scent and special properties which gave it a mixture of cosmetic, medicinal and culinary uses.

According to the Greeks, the rose was the symbol of Aphrodite while the ancient Romans associated it with Venus. A Greek myth tells the story of how Aphrodite, as she ran towards the dying Adonis, was pricked by a rose bush and her blood, as it fell on the petals, dyed them red for eternity. Some say that the blood of Adonis was transformed into red roses while others believe that these flowers reflect the delightful blushes of Venus who was surprised by Jupiter as she was bathing.

The first roses of spring were offered to Venus in wreaths intertwined with myrtle branches during the festival of *Vinalia* in May. During the games held in honour of Flora, the participants had to run while carrying roses, their skill lying in their ability to combine speed while protecting the delicate flowers.

The rose of Paestum bloomed twice a year, a real rarity when it was natural for the plant to have one annual flowering. The rose was widely grown during Roman times and required a special technique for grafting, which is described by

Perfume containers
from Paestum

many ancient authors. In *De rosis nascentibus* the narrator walks at dawn in an irrigated *hortus* or garden and sees wonderful rose gardens created by the skills of the inhabitants of Paestum at cultivating the plants. The expression *Paestano cultu* refers to the special skill of the city's inhabitants in growing roses, an art that created a unique spectacle: the stunning roses had incredibly lush blooms. The most commonly cited attribute of the *bifera* damask rose refers to a context in which the specialised production of the plants continued from spring to autumn with a double flowering. This extraordinary achievement was due to the complex grafts onto different plants and rootstock. The surface of these rose gardens became a sea of purple resembling a royal cloak as a result of the grafts made on plants tied to light canes, as shown in the fresco of the House of the Gold Bracelet in Pompeii. The techniques used at Paestum must have been familiar elsewhere and widely used, to judge from the account given by

Pliny. Referring to Campania, he praised the cultivation of its roses, describing them as plentiful 'cabbage roses' which were beautifully scented and double flowering. This precisely matches the description of the roses from Paestum. In the north-west corner of the forum of Paestum, fair-

Graphic layout
of the exhibition catalogue
Rosantico

ly recent excavations have brought to light a perfumery with an excellently-preserved press used to make olive oil, which was the basic ingredient for preparing ancient perfumes.

the discovery of the site

"I searched here and rapidly began digging in the earth. The temples, which stood firmly rooted to the ground, seemed to mark out the plan of the city but I suspected this was not the case. I searched anxiously beneath this level until, in front of them (the temples), where the known levels finished, other levels appeared in which it was possible to reach the original ancient level of the Greek and Roman city".

Spurred by this intention and with the firm intention of saving the site of the heir to the glorious city of Sybaris from its humiliating isolation, Vittorio Spinazzola travelled to Paestum. Until then, it had been thought that the level on which the temples stood was the lowest level. Instead, through his *anxious searches*, he managed to demonstrate that there were at least two further levels below the level of the columns. What remained of the altars, streets, houses, of everyday life, of the fascinating allure of the place where the Greeks from Sybaris came to

found a new colony with the name of Poseidonia – a precious piece of heritage from the history of humanity – lay below the ground and was still waiting to be excavated. The plain was dotted with just a few scattered farmhouses and, for a long time, the area which is now the archaeological park was engulfed by advancing and insalubrious marshland. It had been almost completely abandoned in favour of the safer and more comfortable hillside of Capaccio.

Around the mid-eighteenth century, Count Felice Gazola, commander of the artillery of the Kingdom of Naples, arrived in the area. The splendid solitude of the temples offered a striking sight. The monumental ruins of the best-preserved religious buildings in Magna Graecia stood out against the horizon and, still today, exert a strong fascination due to the extraordinary effects of the light. The count described the marvel of these buildings to the king and the wider world and made such good drawings of them that Soufflot rewarded his efforts by publishing a successful first edition in Paris. The ruins of these three magnif-

icent ancient buildings had been well-known long before Gazola's work. However, this was the moment when Paestum became the destination for a learned, sophisticated form of tourism. European intellectuals and aristocrats visited its ruins as a vital stage of the *Grand Tour*. The whole city became part of a programme to protect the large monuments of the kingdom. The restoration of the large temples by the architect Bonucci dates back to 1805. Despite the mixed results, the monument that most eloquently reflects the imposing scale of the work is the *athenaion*, also known as the Temple of Ceres. In late antiquity and during the Middle Ages, the building was transformed into a Christian church and subsequently into stables. The walls that blocked off the space between the columns were demolished, recreating the original appearance of the Greek temple. The most catastrophic event to befall the temples took place in 1829: the creation of the road known as the 'road of the Calabrias' (or 'of Tirrena Inferiore'), the main road subsequently known as 'Statale 18'. The road still dissects the city in two, passing through two breaches made in the city walls both to the north and the south. The expropriation of the ancient city followed a selective logic aimed solely at enhancing the part of the city with striking monuments. Of the 120 hectares within the walls, only 25 belong to the state: the central area with the temples, the forum and a few blocks to the west of the large ancient public area.

During the whole of the nineteenth century, there are records of numerous chance excavations and finds, in particular funerary structures, including some of the famous Lucanian tombs painted in the fourth century BC. The excavations of the ancient city, which began in the spring of 1907, unearthed most of the monuments that are currently visible and did not always respect the stratigraphy and the buildings. However, the main excavations took place following the Second World War. Financed by the Cassa del Mezzogiorno (Fund for the South of Italy), the work was not marked by scientific rigour which took second place to the urgent need to find employment in southern Italy.

The period when most attention was focused on the site coincided with the appointment of Mario Napoli as director of the excavations. This marked the beginning of the main phase of research when the amphitheatre and houses were restored.

A programme of systematic excavation of the cemetery began, although it was continuously threatened by clandestine digging. This was the period which saw the discovery of the Tomb of the Diver and the most imposing Lucanian tombs with the richest grave goods. This virtuous phase culminated in an extraordinary crescendo of positive energy which, from 1972, involved constant synergy between research institutions and public organisations. The result is the work of many Italian and foreign scholars who still study, explore and write about the history of the urban planning of the city and the surrounding area.

Giovan Battista Piranesi
**View of the cella
of the Temple of Neptune**

Giovan Battista Lusieri
**View of the temples
of Paestum**
Broomhall, Elgin collection

the **archaeological park**

Although it is no longer the original height, the **city wall** of Paestum is one of the most well-preserved defensive walls in Magna Graecia.

The perimeter, which is trapezoid in shape, is 4,750 metres long, and it possible to follow the whole length of the wall by going along the modern road that skirts round it. The old river Salso, now Capodifiume, lapped against the city walls to the south and filled the ancient moat which, at least on this side, would have been about 11 me-

tres deep and about 20 metres wide. Moving round the whole perimeter of the city walls, it is possible to count 28 towers, placed to defend the gates, some of which are only accessible from the ramparts while others are accessible from within the city. Two of the towers, which are quadrangular, were completely restored in the nineteenth century. The two wall faces, strengthened with masonry piers, were built of blocks of local limestone, and contain a filling of earth and rubble with a thickness ranging from 5 to 6 metres. The whole layout is the result of modifications and restoration, which took place over a period ranging from the 6th to the 1st century BC. There are four gates to the city: **Porta della Giustizia (Justice Gate)**, to the south, **Porta della Marina (Marine Gate)**, to the west, which is the best preserved; **Porta della Sirena (Siren Gate)**, to the east which, beneath the keystone of the round arch, preserves a small relief sculpture of a siren or mermaid, and the **Porta dell'Aurea**

The eastern **wall**

Bronze **vase**
from the Heroon

on pages 28 and 29
Porta Sirena

(Golden Gate), to the north. The latter gate was destroyed when the Bourbon road of the Calabrias was built, cutting the city in two. The road, which is now the route of the former SS 18 road, also caused the destruction of a large stretch of the walls which must have originally been at least seven metres high. The 47 small openings placed along the entire perimeter are posterns which must have been used for the maintenance and defence of the walls.

••••••••••••••••••

the northern temple and the temple of ceres

The temple was bounded to the south by the large road running east/west which separated it from the *agora*, and on the western side of the *plateia* running north/south (no longer visible today), while the eastern and northern boundaries are not clear. The best preserved buildings are the large **temple of Athena (the so-called Temple of Ceres)**, with its altar and the archaic shrine, also presumably dedicated to the goddess of Wisdom. Of the other religious buildings, the remains of another altar, two shrines and a portico are clearly visible. A single towering **column** stands on a base with three steps and was built in the modern era using ancient materials. The Doric temple of Athena, built at

the woman flower

The woman flower was one of the most common votive offerings to be made in the temples of Paestum dating during the fourth century BC. The votive object is unique to the pottery workshops of Paestum where the type originated. During sacred rituals it would have been used as a censer. Made of terracotta, the women flowers consist of the bust or just the head of a woman topped by the calyx of a bell-shaped flower, the wild lily that still grows on the sand dunes of Cilento. There are many different variants of this type of votive object, some of which are extremely elaborate. Large numbers of them have been found in all the temples of the city and the surrounding area.

3

Flower women
from the Temple of Foce Sele

the end of the sixth century BC, was made of local limestone. Imposing columns surrounded the *cella* that housed the cult statue.

At the end of the 1990s the building underwent complex conservative restoration which made it possible to identify, at several points, traces of the painted stucco-work that highlighted the ornate decorative features. The traditional name of the building, associated with the goddess Ceres, dates back to the eighteenth century. Many scholars have ascribed it to a note by the great architectural historian Vitruvius who stated that the goddess was worshipped by the Greeks in front of the gates of the city. The temple was actually dedicated to Athena as is shown by the votive offerings, in particular the small terracotta figurines, which are on display in the museum in the section devoted to the temple, depicting the divinity from the early archaic period.

The entablature of the temple consisted of a smooth architrave, decorated only with moulding of *ovoli* (instead of the canonical smooth fillet), the Doric frieze and the cornice. After going through the outer columns (*peristasi*) on the eastern front, one comes to the *cella*, but only after passing through the vestibule, preceded by four Ionic columns on the front and the two on the sides. The only surviving traces of this colonnade are the bases, several fragments of columns still in situ and two capitals kept in the nearby museum. Nothing is preserved of the *cella* except for the floor, which is a metre higher than the external colonnade. The use of two architectural orders, Doric for the outer columns and Ionic for the inner ones, and the mixture of elements of the elevation, make the building one of the most accomplished examples of late archaic temple architecture. The temple continued to maintain its cult function, even after the city became a Latin colony in 273 BC when there is an inscription dedicated to Minerva, the Roman equivalent of Athena. The altar is situated about 30 metres from the façade. All that remains of the altar is the stone podium and a few parts of the elevation. Immediately to the south east, the foundations of the oldest building in the city are preserved. They are presumably the remains of the first shrine to Athena. Beautiful terracotta elements, found during the excavations in the 1930s, were part of the original decoration. Now on display in the museum, they are some of the best-preserved eaves in all the monuments in the city. If observed carefully, it will be seen that the back of the slabs still have painted letters which were used to ensure their correct assembly.

on pages 32 and 33
The **Temple of Ceres**

1

....
the agora

The term 'agora' refers to the **public space and meeting area** in ancient Greek cities. It was a distinctive part of Greek urban architecture and functioned as the central square and the religious centre of the city, with both political and civic buildings. From the fifth century BC, the public area in Paestum was filled with buildings whose plans are not always particularly clear. They were often rearranged in later eras, such as the *heroon*, or even demolished when the city became a Latin colony, as happened with the *ekklesiasterion* or the assembly building. As well as these monuments, there are other buildings which belong topographically to the *agora*: the archaic shrine, the so-called Shrine of Chiron, the square building, the shrine of Zeus Agoraios, the building with the kiln, the shrine/*naiskos*, the *asklepieion*, the amphiprostyle shrine, the temple of Demeter, the altars of these religious buildings, the so-called banqueting room and the large temples. Certain public functions were also performed in the two *stoai*: these were colonnaded buildings, generally with one or two naves, which were designed as a shelter for the faithful in the large temples or public complexes. The whole area, which would later be occupied partly by the Roman forum, has a complex stratigraphy and its boundaries have still not been clearly defined. The square of the future forum of Paestum has underwent a radical transformation and the buildings that formed the Greek agora were largely razed to the ground with the onset of Romanisation.

the ekklesiasterion

The **ekklesiasterion**
citizens' assembly hall

2

The oldest building in the agora dates to about 480-470 BC. Its steps, made from the natural outcrop of rock, form a circular structure with concentric rings. Entirely carved out of the rock, it is now clearly visible below the temple which had been built over the structure in Roman times. In the upper part of the building the structure has a diameter of about 35 metres while it measures 9 metres in the lowest part. On the western side the remaining part of the stone seats covering the tiers and the small altar they enclosed are still well-preserved.

The ekklesiasterion was built by the inhabitants of Poseidonia **for meetings of the assembly of citizens** who voted for the laws and elected the magistrates. It could seat from 1100 to 1700 people and continued to be used by the Lucanians for their institutions. The monument was used until at least the third century BC and one of the last pieces of material evidence for its functions is a limestone stele coated in plaster with a painted inscription in red lettering. Written in Oscan, the language spoken by the Lucanians, it describes a dedication to Jupiter 'for

3 The **heroon**
510 a.C.

the heroon

In ancient Greek colonies, the **heroon** was a building dedicated to the cult of a hero or a heroised figure. It occupied an area in the agora and generally contained the mortal remains – whether real or presumed – of the founder of the city. At Paestum the monument stands inside a rectangular enclosure made of stone blocks which contains a small rectangular building, with three walls carved out of the rock and a fourth constructed wall. The building has two roofs, an older one made of stone slabs and another one made of tiles. It has no entrance. Three of the inner walls are plastered, while at the centre of the structure there is a sort of stone table, made by placing one block of stone on top of another. There were five long iron spits with leather handles. Six *hydriai*, vases generally used to contain water, two bronze amphorae displaying exquisite workmanship and an attic black figure vase portraying the triumph of Hercules, were arranged along the walls. The vases contained honey which is still preserved, mainly in lumps.

The construction of the building dates to around the end of the sixth century BC, the period when the stone roof and the earthern mound covering it were built. The rectangular enclosure and the

favours received' and can be dated to around 300 BC.

With the arrival of the Romans, the building was demolished and completely buried by a large midden of earth, stones and bones, the remains of an ancient sacrifice. A temple was built on the top of the mound, although no trace remains of the deity who was worshipped there. It is still possible to make out the rectangular enclosure, marked by a small colonnade, and the fountain which now stands on a modern brick support.

tile roof date to a rearrangement that can be dated to about the mid-third century BC. The current appearance of the area dates to the period when the city became a Latin colony: the mound was removed, the sacred building was placed within a rectangular enclosure made of stone blocks and the space inside was filled with earth.

Remnants of the **curia**
1st century AD

10

··················

the aerarium, the comitium and the curia

To the south of the amphitheatre, there is a much older rectangular building made of large blocks of stone which is clearly visible. Due to its position with respect to the *comitium*, the building has been identified as the city's **aerarium** (treasury). Datable to the third century BC, it is one of the first buildings of the Latin colony and revenues and administrative deeds were kept here. A short distance from this building, there are traces of the most important public monument of the Latin colony: the **comitium**. It was used for meetings of the *curias* when elections were held to elect the magistrates of the colony and judicial hearings also took place here. It consisted of a tiered *cavea* within a square enclosure. On the northern side, the building adjoins the large rooms of the curia to which there was direct ac-

7 The **amphitheatre**
1st century AD - 2nd century AD.

cess from the tiers. The **bronze statue of Marsyas** can also be associated with the *comitium*. Currently on display in the museum, it was found in a part of the forum near a brick structure identified as the altar of *Lares Compitales*.

The current appearance of the **curia** corresponds to the most recent phase of the building dating to the first century BC: a rectangular building with a semi-circular stone bench in the centre. In this sector, the survey of the structures identified so far have enabled scholars to recognise the complexity of the events surrounding the transformation of the agora into the forum.

the temple of peace

The building, which occupied a central part of the forum, dates to between the second and first centuries BC. Built partly on the *comitium*, it is generally known as the **Temple of Peace**. There is debate about the attribution: some scholars believe it was the temple of the Capitoline Triad, others argue it was the *Capitolium* of the city, while the building has also been attributed to the *Dioscuri*.

It is possible to enter the monument from the central steps which lead to the large podium of the building. The area occupied by the sacred building still preserves part of the elevation which is aligned on the podium. By walking on this side of the forum, it is possible to admire some of the monumental Corinthian capitals, the architraves and the Doric frieze, and the carved metopes which recount the sacking of the sanctuary of Delphi by the Gauls. According to scholars, the *cella* housed the statue of Bona Mens, the goddess associated with freedmen's gratitude towards their former masters. The goddess played an important role in the religious life of the city during Roman times.

the amphitheatre

Although only the western half has been excavated and is visible today, the **amphitheatre** at Paestum is divided in two parts by the Bourbon road of the Calabrias, now the main road SS 18. Built in the first century AD, it was extended between the late first and the early second century AD. The load-bearing walls and the *cavea* belong to the oldest phase and were made of large blocks of limestone. The pilasters, supports and arches were built of brick and, leaning against the load-bearing wall, provided easy access to the wooden tribunes. This arena, like other similar buildings, was used for circus shows and gladiatorial displays. The tunnel that led into the amphitheatre is still intact and accessible and would have been used for transporting animals, props and sets for the shows.

Like the **theatre**, this building played a vital part in the life of all important Roman cities. In the amphitheatres, the *munera gladiatoria* (a gladiatorial contest) were often sponsored by wealthy people who put on public shows at their own expense to celebrate special events or festivals.

····················
the forum

In Roman cities, the **forum area** was the heart of city life. The forum at Paestum measured about 200 metres from east to west and about 60 metres from north to south. In its present guise, the forum is the result of the layout carried out in Augustan times when the colonnades surrounding the square were built and the floor level was lowered. The area was surrounded on all sides by buildings used to commerce: the *tabernae* or shops, the covered market and the *macellum*. By looking carefully, it is still possible to distinguish important political buildings such as the *comitium*, the curia and the *tabularium* or city archive, judicial buildings such as the Basilica, religious buildings such as the so-called temple of Peace and the *sacella* (small shrines). A short stretch of basalt road, with its wide pavements, skirts round the amphitheatre and leads the visitor to the forum area. Built after the city became a Latin colony in 273 BC, it was used for a long time and by walking along part of it, it is still possible to pass by the *comitium*, the *aerarium* and the shops. The *macellum* lies on the other side of the forum. The most intriguing part of this part of the site are the **shops**, some retaining the original flooring which has been covered to protect them from wear and weathering. A

portico dating to one of the final phases prior to the city's abandonment houses the shops on the northern and southern sides. Built according to almost identical modules, the shops are divided into two rooms - the front and back of the shops – and stand directly on the natural bedrock. Some of them have traces of staircases and would therefore have been at least two storey buildings and they also have a pit for the disposal of rubbish. A wide

The Roman **forum**

range of activities took place in the buildings: one of the most accurately studied shops has an olive press which has led archaeologists to interpret the building as a perfumer's. At the centre of the shops there is a *lararium*, or **temple of the Lares,** built of brick, considered by scholars to be more recent than the layout of the forum. The forum leads to the *macellum* or **market** by means of a staircase that enables visitors to walk on the oldest level of the courtyard and the area surrounded by shops. Walls and the remains of superimposing structures make it difficult to visit the monument and prevent full understanding of the phases that led to the current layout which dates to late Imperial times.

the residential districts

A large part of the western sector of the city is occupied by residential districts. The result of constant transformations that took place throughout the history of the city, the area contains buildings with different features and dimensions. Of the eight blocks which have been completely brought to light, seven are almost identical in size: they are extremely long, measuring 273 metres. They have a north/south orientation and contain houses and small passageways that run east/west between the blocks. The residential structures that can be visited today and are the best-preserved have undergone enlargements and transformations which have radically altered the original structure, sometimes damaging nearby houses and public streets. Of the various structures that can be visited today, the part that is now visible dates to the late Imperial period, the final phase of use.

Of the various *domus* open to visitors, one of the most interesting is the **house with the swimming pool**. It extends for about 2,500 square metres and is divided into numerous rooms. The main feature of this large *domus* is the spacious pool or swimming pool, dating to the Imperial period, which is surrounded by a large peristyle with brick columns. Its functions and the layout of the surrounding rooms are still being studied. The **house with peristyle and thermal baths** is situated in the block immediately to the west of the former *domus*. This house contains the rooms of a small thermal bath and include the following: the room with a pool for cold baths (*frigidarium*), the pool for warm baths (*tepidarium*), the pool for hot baths (*calidarium*) and the remains of the heating system (*praefurnium*).

the pool or temple dedicated to fortuna virilis

A walk behind the forum takes you to an enormous area enclosed by a wall. The complex, known as the **temple with natatio or pool**, was made of local stone covered on the bottom and on the pilasters with *cocciopesto*. It can be dated to the first phase of the Latin colony and thus to the third century BC. Access to the structure, which measures 47 x 21 metres, is provided by a ramp and there are a series of pilasters at the end which would have supported a wooden platform. Scholars have argued that the temple was linked to a ritual called *Veneralia*, well known from the ancient sources, and to fertility rites, suggesting that Fortuna Virilis, the deity worshipped here, derived

The **pool** or temple
dedicated to Fortuna Virilis
3rd century BC

View of the **pool** area

4

12 **13** View of the area of the **Basilica** and the **Temple of Neptune**

directly from Venus. Ovid describes the main phases of these ceremonies which ceased to be held after the early Imperial period, when the structure was partly buried to make space for other buildings: the *Caesareum* and the gymnasium. During the religious ceremony the sides of the pool marked the enclosure within which the procession took place. The statue of the deity was lowered into the water to help married women, without distinction of rank or social status, to have a safe delivery. The cult statue, which at the end of the ceremony was placed on a wooden platform (supported by pilasters that are still visible), was then celebrated with a clothing ceremony and decorated with flowers and jewels.

the thermal baths

Between the edge of the southern temple, the so-called Roman garden and to the north of the shops in the forum, it is possible to observe the ruins of the **public baths**, whose entrance was on the street running north/south. Made of limestone blocks, small bricks and mortar, the building can be dated to the late Imperial period, presumably around the first half of the third century AD. Although only a few parts of the wall decoration are known, it is extremely likely that the structure, like other similar buildings in other Roman cities, was elaborately adorned with marbles and paintings. Along the walls, it is possible to make out the heating system made of terracotta pipes and small pilasters that support the floor, just like modern thermal baths. The system enabled the air and water, heated in a *praefurnium*, to circulate and reach the building from a cistern situated on the eastern side. It is fairly simple to discern the *apodyterium* or changing room, the *calidarium* or room for hot baths, the *frigidarium* or room for cold baths, and the *tepidarium* or room for warm baths.

the southern temple

The temple was bounded to the north by the large road running east/west while the northern limit was marked by the *plateia* running north/south. Close to the *macellum*, it is possible to make out the foundations of an arch which presumably constituted the monumental entrance in Roman times. The most well-preserved buildings are the large **Temple of Neptune** with its altar and **the so-called Basilica, dedicated to the goddess Hera** with its altar.

Not far from the temples, there is a row of **fourteen altars**, not all contemporary with each other, of which only the foundations are preserved. The last one to the south has been dated to the late republican period while the others date to the fifth and fourth centuries BC. Identifying the different structures in the area is a particularly challenging task. The most well-preserved buildings are the **shrine to Mater Matuta**, which can be dated to the third century BC and a circular structure, just visible beneath the *macellum*, which has been identified as the **Temple of Hercules**. The entire area, associated with cults that were established after the foundation of the Latin colony, was separated from the southern temple by a small cement wall. Part of the **temple**

12 The **Temple of Neptune** and the **Basilica** in the background

13

dedicated to the cult of Asclepius can be seen almost next to the modern road. Two rows of rooms to the north and south can be seen in the courtyard, surrounded by porticoes and fountains, while the eastern side, which must have provided the monumental entrance to the building, still lies below the road surface. The rites took place in the courtyard and only subsequently did the sick person enter the large room with the platform which was the most sacred part of the whole complex. The

monument can be dated to about 300 BC and was transformed into a farm during the late Roman period.

Lastly, to the west of the altars and close to the oldest boundary wall of the so-called **"Roman garden"**, a rectangular area situated behind the *macellum*, there is a **shrine**. Commonly known as the "amphiprostyle" (with columns both on the front and the rear facades), the shrine has its own altar. The building is linked to the Lucanian phase of the colony and is associated with the cult of Hercules. Most of the other buildings incorporated within the perimeter of the temple are still being studied. Another interesting structure, situated to the west of the Basilica, is the **so-called water clock**. The building, which can be dated to the fourth century BC, has once more become the focus of archaeological interest. The rectangular podium covered in limestone flooring, the remains of wells, guttering and the likelihood that there was a room with a roof supported by columns, have led archaeologists to believe that the structure was a *hestiatorion*. Used for banquets and collective meals, similar buildings are widespread in numerous sacred areas both in Greece and in Greek temples in southern Italy.

....
the temple of neptune

The **Temple of Neptune**, built in the mid-fifth century BC, is one of the most well-preserved Doric buildings in Magna Graecia. Made of local limestone, the building's attribution is still uncertain. Its imposing columns appear to be lighter due to the thick series of grooves carved into the shafts. The sharp edges create effects of light and shadow and give the columns a bulkiness that makes them look like the folds of a *peplos*, the traditional dress worn by Greek women. The frieze consisted of triglyphs and uncarved metopes. The walls of the *cella*, which

Terracotta statue
of male deity
seated on a throne [Zeus?]
c. 520 BC

4

housed the statue of the god, have been completely destroyed; the interior is divided into three naves by two rows of columns, arranged on two floors. The staircases on both sides of the *cella* provided access to the wooden roof, facilitating maintenance work. Some scholars believe the building was dedicated to Zeus or to Apollo, while others

12 The **Temple of Neptune** and the **Basilica**

13

13 The **Basilica**
530 BC

temple while the nearer one is Roman and dates to the late republican period.

think it was associated with the cult of Hera. The ancient Greeks were not content merely to apply mathematical precision to architectural features. They also attached great importance to visual perfection. They therefore made a series of imperceptible optical adjustments to the temple so that the appearance, and not just the architecture, appeared to be perfect. To the east of the temple there are two altars of different sizes and date. The more distant of the two is contemporary with the

....
the basilica

The name stems from the lack of pediments which led eighteenth century scholars to believe that the building had civic functions: although they have been lost, it is still possible to see the architectural terracotta features that covered the wooden roof which have been partly preserved and reconstructed in the museum.

Later transformed into a Christian church,

the building has a distinctive façade due to the odd number of columns, a sign of the archaic origins of the temple, together with the *entasis* and the accentuated tapering of the columns. Compared to those in the nearby temple of Neptune, the capitals are much flatter. The *cella* is divided into two parts by a portico. This typology of building is thought to have had a ritual character and has led some scholars to suggest the presence of two cults in the building. It can be dated to 530 BC. Judging from the inscriptions and *ex votos* found in the area, the **temple was dedicated to Hera and possibly to Zeus**. The statue of the god, reconstruct-ed from numerous fragments and now on display in the museum, comes from the area between the so-called Temple of Neptune and the northern boundary of the temple. Careful comparison of the individual elements of these two large buildings makes it possible to follow the various events that marked the consolidation of the Doric order over a period of about seventy years.

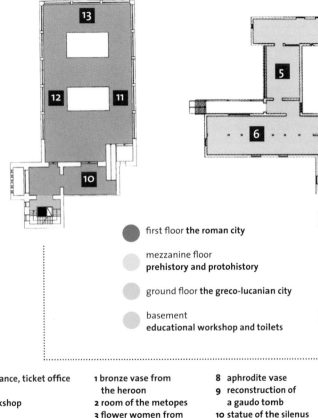

the national archaeological museum

first floor **the roman city**

mezzanine floor
prehistory and protohistory

ground floor **the greco-lucanian city**

basement
educational workshop and toilets

a entrance, ticket office

b bookshop

c exhibition area

d educational area

1 bronze vase from
  the heroon
2 room of the metopes
3 flower women from
  the temples
4 statue of male deity
  seated on a throne [zeus?]
5 tomb of the diver
6 painted lucanian tombs
7 vase by assteas portraying
  rape of europa

8 aphrodite vase
9 reconstruction of
  a gaudo tomb
10 statue of the silenus
  marsyas
11 reliefs decorated
  with plant motifs
12 portrait of tiberius
13 female statues
  of saint venera

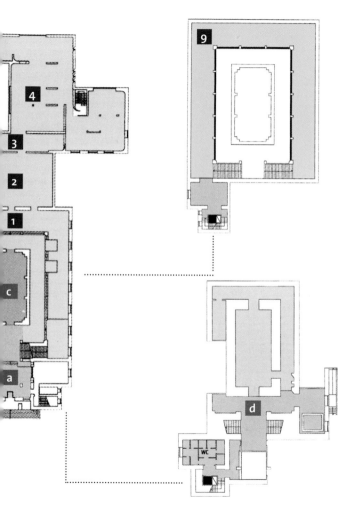

the **museum**

The Museum provides a vivid portrait and reconstruction of the identity and long-term transformations of the archaeological site. Visitors can admire the rich finds that have emerged over the centuries from the extraordinary mixture of temples, civic residences and public places, shrines, tombs, theatres and natural 'man-made' environments.

Based on the ambitious design of Maurizio De Vita (1938), the museum opened in 1952 and is situated in the heart of the ancient city walls. It provides a linear presentation of the four crucial periods in the life of the city of Paestum and the surrounding area, from prehistory to the osmosis and discon-

5

Tomb of the Diver
Symposium
470 BC

tinuities of Greek, Lucanian and Roman civilisations: the collection ranges from the most ancient finds, the **room of the metopes** from the temple of Hera at the mouth of the river Sele, to the **painted tombs**, first displayed from the 1960s; at the centre is the icon of eternity, a journey of discovery featuring musical banquets, games and the mystery of death, engraved on the **stone slabs of the Diver**; the elegant grave goods include everyday objects, **bronze vases**, pottery and aristocratic status symbols. There also displays of collections of material related to the Lucanian civilisation. More recent displays include the section devoted to **prehistory**, on the mezzanine floor, and the rooms on the first floor provide a succinct overview of **Roman Paestum**; these rooms complete the museum itinerary which explores memory and stratified identities.

An undisputed masterpiece of Italic black figure pottery is the **krater portraying the rape of Europa**, made by the potter Asteas (who was

Mezzanine floor
Prehistoric and protohistoric
section

9 Reconstruction
of a **Gaudo tomb**

active at Paestum in about the mid-fourth century BC); the vase returned to Paestum in 2009 after an adventurous journey which took it as far as Malibu. The vase tells the story of Europa, the daughter of the king of the Phoenicians, and Zeus. In order to overcome Europa's reluctance, Zeus turns himself into a gentle white bull who drags her out to sea as far as the island of Crete where the wedding is celebrated in the presence of divine accomplices.

····················
prehistory and protohistory

This is one of the most recent sections in the museum and is dedicated to the memory of the archaeologist Gianni Bailo Modesti, who died prematurely and had curated its design and the layout. The ancient settlement of the Sele plain is described through reconstructions and information panels which describe the main phases from the Palaeolithic to the early Iron Age. The phase with the richest evidence is the Neolithic which at Paestum is represented by the Gaudo culture.

In 1943 the Allies landed in the Bay of Salerno and, in order to organise their general headquarters, began to excavate in the Gaudo area to make a runway for the air forces. During the work, Lieutenant J.G.S. Brinson, who was an ar-chaeologist, was asked to intervene. He carried out rigorous excavations of the first of a series of **prehistoric tombs** and arranged for the earth-moving work to be undertaken elsewhere, thus saving one of the most important prehistoric funerary sites in Italy. This is a crucial chronological phase for the study of prehistoric cultures: the multiple Gaudo burials tell the story of the first groups of people in the area who decided to live in stable communities. The tombs, of which a careful reconstruction can be seen in the museum, consisted of one or two chambers, hewn from the bank of tuff and linked to each other by a shaft. The tombs are full of a wide variety of **ceramic finds** which often reproduce,

without the use of the potter's wheel, objects which in everyday life would have been made of perishable materials. The tombs were used for multiple burials and the funeral rites were held there, as is shown by the remains of animal bones and the fragments of bits of clay used to produce pottery objects specially for the occasion. The Bronze Age is represented only by a few objects found in the area of the future city of Paestum and the **bronze axes** which were discovered in a settlement situated close to the future 'Porta Giustizia' (Justice Gate). The grave goods found at Arenosola and at Tempalta are associated with the Iron Age communities of the Villanovan culture which marked their territory on this side of the river Sele.

··················
assteas's workshop

The Museum of Paestum houses the largest collection of red figure vases attributed to local workshops, dating from the late fifth century to the early third century BC.

Of the various craftsmen who made vases in Paestum, there are two artists who stand out. This is because with they renewed a much older tradition that was popular in archaic and classical Athens and proudly signed their most imposing works. The signature is either engraved or painted with white paint and is always placed along the same axis as the main part of the representation. The artists were named Python and Assteas. The latter artisan is the most famous potter from Paestum: his workshop, which was active in the city between 375-350 BC, produced numerous vases, both signed and unsigned, which are now kept in the leading museums of the world. It is often impossible to match them to the original grave goods but the provenance from the cemetery of Paestum is certain.

Of the twelve signed objects known to specialists, two are on display in the Museum of Paestum: the **hydria with the myth of Bellerophon** formed part of the rich funerary goods from the painted chamber tomb found in the hills of Agropoli, while the **krater of Europa and the bull** was discovered in the cemetery of Sant'Agata dei Goti and restored to the nation's heritage thanks to the careful investigations of the Nucleo Tutela Patrimonio Culturale (Cultural Heritage Squad) of the Carabinieri.

Assteas was a creative and hard-working craftsman who mainly signed large works decorated with mythological scenes. The scenes were often linked to

7

on pages 61, 62, 63
Vase portraying the **Rape of Europa**
signed by **Assteas**
375-350 BC

the world of the ancient theatre, which is sometimes evoked in the portrayals, partly through the inclusion of wooden features and stage sets and props used for shows and plays. A constant feature of his work is the combination of mythological themes, as described in literary texts, and the Dionysian world, according to a principle that regulates the transmission of images in all the pottery made at Paestum for funerary purposes. The myth is very accurately told through the portrayal on the main scene of the vase. The characters are always identified with their name written alongside. This reflects a craft tradition that is perfectly at home with the most learned and sophisticated aspects of mythological storytelling, a principle shared by many of the non-Greek communities of southern Italy.

....
the pottery workshops at paestum: the aphrodite painter

The **amphora of the Aphrodite painter** is one of the most beautifully painted "sculptural" portrayals of lush vegetation to frame a figurative scene. Since its discovery, these features have made the amphora an exceptional example of pottery decoration within the context of Magna Graecia and the workshops of Paestum. The vase comes from a female cist tomb, no. 13 from the Licinella cemetery at Paestum. There were eleven vessels among the grave goods and all the painted vessels, except for the *lekane* and the dish decorated with fish, belonged to the same workshop which Greco identified and Trendall named. The choice of name inevitably fell upon the figure who personalised the main scenes of the three most important vases from the tomb: Aphrodite. The goddess is portrayed in three themes commonly associated with her: the epiphany of the goddess, the judgement of Paris and the story of Aphrodite and Dionysus. The craftsman who made the objects that would accompany the deceased in the afterlife is unanimously considered to be a painter from Paestum. He would have trained in workshops in Apulia which were renowned for their constant and skillful use of polychrome

8 *on pages 65, 66, 67*
Amphora by the
Aphrodite painter
330 BC

pottery. This is the phase when plant decoration is transformed into three-dimensional bouquets of leaves and brightly coloured flowers of which there are hundreds on the surface of the vase. The motifs have a fresh, spontaneous feel and were initially used as decoration of the less important parts of the vase although they gradually became the basis for a new, lively and realistic portrayal of nature. The symbolic character is quite clear although its precise meaning is hard to decipher. According to scholars, its origins can be traced to the depiction of volumes used in great painting. The large space devoted by the craftsman to these these decorative schemes stems from the desire to portray nature: the ribbons, tendrils and spirals that frame

the group of birds almost become the protagonists of the scene. Their composition is reminiscent of delicate embroidery and they fill up the large body of the amphora, connecting the birth of a deity with the Dionysian setting that develops on the other side of the monumental vase in a harmonious whole. As will be seen by observing the vases on display in the museum, Aphrodite and Dionysus (the deities associated with flowers) often symbolise the constant motion of re-flowering and the continuous return to life.

···················
the metopes from the temple at the mouth of the river sele

The **metopes from the Temple of Hera Argiva, situated at the mouth of the river Sele**, constitute one of the most important examples of archaic decorative stone cycles from the ancient world. Dating to about 570-560 BC, they are either made in relief or are simply shown in outline, using local sandstone. They are on display in a part of the museum that was supposed to facilitate understanding, although they often tend to confuse visitors because they appear to belong to a single religious structure. Found in a ditch where they had been dumped, they are still hard to interpret. There is scholarly debate

8 Amphora by the **Aphrodite painter**, detail 330 BC

about their original position within the religious buildings linked to the temple which was identified, excavated and published in a wonderful volume by Umberto Zanotti Bianco and Paola Zancani Montuoro. The area where they were discovered - one of the most famous and important temples in the Greek colonial world – is now accompanied by a modern narrative museum which recounts the functions, position and mythical representations of these splendid works by the artists and artisans of Magna Graecia. The scenes portrayed are taken from the world of the Greek epic and mainly regard episodes from the Trojan War, such as the famous one illustrating the suicide of Ajax and the tasks of Hercules, the hero who was a favourite of Hera.

Dancing girls
metope from the Temple
of Hera at Foce Sele
570-560 BC

······

the oldest cemeteries

The urban cemeteries of Poseidonia are situated in the area of the city immediately to the north and south of the city walls. First explored in the early twentieth century, excavations have revealed a large number of burials which have enabled scholars to identify the transformations in the rites and organisation of funerary areas, from the earliest phases of the Achaean colony. A carefully arranged selection, on display in the rooms of the ground floor of the museum, enables visitors to grasp the differences in the rituals and un-

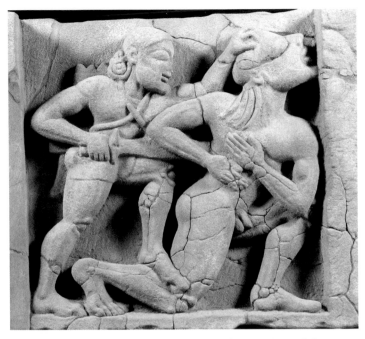

2 **Heracles kills the giant Alcyoneus**
metope from the Temple
of Hera at Foce Sele
570-560 BC

derstand the complex social structure of the inhabitants of this area.

The oldest tombs consist of a large number of imported objects and are extremely austere in character. From the second half of the fifth century BC, different burial practices emerged, linked to a change in the selection of objects that accompanied the voyage of the deceased. These differences reflect the presence of the Lucanians. **Weapons, armour, helmets and greaves** are found in the burials of high-ranking males; elaborately made red figure vases, the work of the most famous potters active in Paestum, indicate the high status of the deceased women. Next to these tombs there is also an anomalous burial which was found at the edge of a graveyard situated about 500 metres north west of the city. The **cist tomb** has a covering slab made of local sandstone, carved with the image of a male face, placed where the face of the corpse would have been. Marina Cipriani, who has studied the cemetery and the context, has suggested that the deceased may have been a shamanic figure linked to a group of warriors, possibly mercenaries, who settled on the edge of the ancient city. The most famous tomb from Paestum comes from a small suburban cemetery: the deceased evidently wanted to bring with him the enigmatic image of a dive and, ever since its discovery in 1968, it has become one of the most renowned images of diving in the world.

the tomb of the diver

On 3 June 1968, in the Tempa del Prete district 1.5 km south of Poseidonia, Mario Napoli excavated a small cemetery and discovered the only known archaic Greek tomb with figurative scenes in Paestum. The archaeologist mentions a second tomb of the same type which was only plastered and lacked grave goods, identified and excavated in the same area. The Tomb of the Diver is a cist tomb that can be dated to 470 BC. The main slab is decorated with the famous scene of the diver while the lateral slabs show a scene of a symposium. The participants at the symposium are

Reconstruction of the **Tomb of the Diver**

5

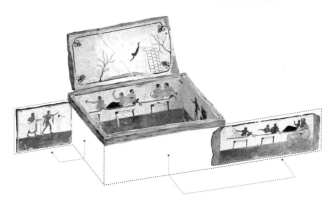

Tomb of the Diver
covering slab
470 BC

portrayed in the final phase of the banquet when they abandon themselves to the pleasures of wine, eroticism, music, song and the game of *kottabos*, which consisted in skillfully flinging drops of wine at other cups: the complex group of objects has always been considered the expression of a rigorous formal logic, reflecting profound psychological insight. Painted on a layer of fresh plaster by two craftsmen, the figures show the presence of a preparatory drawing, made using a sharpened instrument, which formed the basis of the figurative composition. All scholars agree that the main scene is symbolic and the dive should not be interpreted as a real situation –a simple feat of athleticism - but rather as an indication of a metaphorical transition from life to death. Those who support an iconological interpretation of the visual narrative argue that the scenes reflect a cultural milieu whose deepest roots lie in learned poetry and mythology. According to this view, there is a link between the symposium and the dive, demonstrating that the convivial experience of the symposium, the uninhibited nature of the occasion caused by music and love, can be compared to diving into a sea of a different dimension of knowledge. The status of the person buried in this tomb, which belongs to a small settlement inhabited

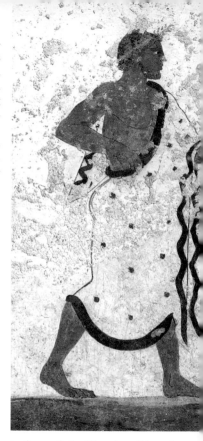

to the south, is still unclear. It is probably the burial of a member of a family group who did not have full citizenship.

on pages 74, 75, 76, 77
Tomb of the Diver
Symposium
470 BC

5

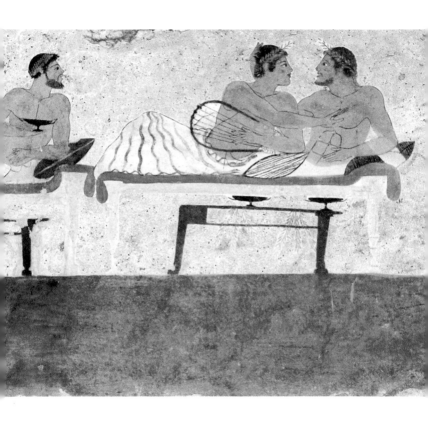

the lucanian cemeteries

Of the roughly thousand **Lucanian tombs** currently known, only about eighty, reserved for a limited and distinct group within the social structure, have painted walls on the interior. The leading groups of the Lucanian city chose, selected and commissioned a series of images that have enabled scholars to study this collection of paintings as though they were a written document. Given the lack of literary texts, they shed light on aspects of the behaviour, mindsets and forms of representation of the Lucanians in Paestum. The tombs were discovered intact. Together with the selection of objects that make up the grave goods of the deceased (on display beside the stone slabs), the tombs recount the complex history of the Lucanian city. All the **paintings at Paestum** were made using a technique similar to that of frescoes: a thin layer of plaster was applied to the slab, carved from local limestone which was polished on the painted side. Agnes Rouveret and Angela Pontrandolfo, who have studied these contexts, have identified the system of representation which focuses on the expression of male values. From 380 BC onwards, the most prestigious tombs were painted with one of the most famous and commonly used scenes: the return of the warrior who always occupies the slab placed behind the head of the deceased. The image, which appears exclusively in male burials, is that of a bearded horseman wearing armour, which is sometimes found in the tomb and was actually worn by the deceased, and carrying spears from which war booty hangs. The image is always associated with functional vessels used for wine drinking, in particular the krater. The warrior, portrayed sitting astride a horse, is celebrated as he returns victorious to his community, and is welcomed by the woman who offers him the vessels for the libation.

In the mid-fourth century BC, an exclusively female figurative programme of decoration was formulated: the woman is seated, intent on spinning yarn, attended by a standing maidservant or else is shown lying on her deathbed

**Tomb 58
from Andriuolo**
340-330 BC

on page 80
**Tomb 58
from Andriuolo**
4th century BC

on page 81
**Tomb 47
from Andriuolo**
360-350 BC

6

12 Portrait of Tiberius
1st century AD

11 Relief decorated
with plant motifs
1st century BC

while being prepared for the funeral or during the funeral itself. However, it was during the second half of the fourth century BC that the desire to create a continuous narrative became evident in all the craft workshops.

During the transitional period from the fourth to the third century BC there was a significant drop in the number of painted tombs. This was a phase that saw renewed tensions between Rome, the Samnites and the Greek cities, and the tombs from this period have exclusively ornamental motifs: figurative scenes are rare. This change has been attributed to a gradual closure of the elite group that led to a new aristocracy whose ideology can be observed in the images in the chamber tombs at the cemetery of Spinazzo, on display in the educational part of the museum of Paestum. This is the cemetery that has the most painted chamber tombs and the ratio between painted tombs (7) and the total number of tombs found (120) suggests there was a restricted oligarchy that controlled the city at the end of the fourth century BC.

....
the roman section

An entire floor of the museum of Paestum is devoted to the episodes concerning the layout and architecture of Paestum and the transformations the city underwent following the foundation of the Latin colony in 273 BC. As is clear from a visit to the city, the most radical transformations concerned the public area and its related monuments. The Greek buildings that had distinguished the identity of the colonies from Sybaris were demolished or used for other purposes in order to give a new look to the heart of the city. The inscriptions related to the leading posts in the city reflect this desire for change and add a personalised touch to the small buildings and fountains in the forum area. Continuity of cult practice is only evident in the sacred areas of the city: **small statues of the Roman goddess Minerva** have been found in the northern temple as well as proof of coexistence with other cults, such as that of Dionysus, known as Liber by the Latin colonists. The southern temple has yielded anatomical **votive statuettes**, found among the votive offerings below the republican temple of the so-called Temple of Neptune, which have been linked to the cult of Apollo; the **statuettes of women riding peacocks with large drums** in

their right hands are related to rituals linked to the worship of Magna Mater. A similar number of objects associated with Latin cults practiced in the shrines of Roman date have been found in the north-west corner of the southern temple. One extremely interesting sector is devoted to the **inscriptions** that record the posts held by leading Lucanian figures. This evidence helps to define the political and social framework of the colony at Paestum. Several **male portraits** and a **hoard** made up of 647 silver *denarii* date to the late republic.

The restoration of the temple of Mens Bona, the so-called Italic temple and the Basilica was organised by the wife of Caius Cocceius Flaccus. Finds from the building include stone material and the only **portrait statue** of her family to be preserved. Private residences of the Imperial period have also provided important sculptural furnishings that decorated the large gardens of the *domus*. There are several sculptures from the Flavian age, including a particularly notable example made in Attica which, according to some scholars, is a portrait of the emperor **Giordan III**.

marsyas

The **bronze statue** has been dated to the second quarter of the third century BC and portrays the Silenus Marsyas in shackles. According to several scholars, it is a copy of a statue erected by the plebeians in Rome in the most important area of the forum. The presence of the statue in the forum at Paestum has a special significance, given the symbolic value of the myth regarding the unfortunate character. Pindar tells the story of his talent and the exemplary punishment that Apollo devised for him. Marsyas was highly skilled at playing the *aulos*, a musical instrument similar to a flute which the goddess Athena had thrown away after inventing it since her cheeks were deformed when she played it. Homer tells the story of how capricious and irascible the gods could be and Marsyas, often portrayed as ugly and deformed, would not escape their wrath.

As soon as Athena abandoned the instrument, Marsyas was seized by curiosity so he picked it up and started to play it. The melody he managed to produce was so delightful that everyone was enchanted. Those who heard him play could never forget the celestial sound of his *aulos*, even comparing his talent to the god Apollo. When the god heard about Marsyas's fame, he could not bear the idea that anyone should be considered better than him so he challenged Marsyas to a contest. The Muses were appointed judges of the contest and the prize-winner was entitled to do whatever he wanted with the defeated adversary. Thanks to a cunning stratagem, Apollo emerged the winner and his revenge was cruel. He decided to punish Marsyas for his arrogance so he tied him to a tree and flayed him alive.

Bronze statue
of the silenus **Marsyas**
3rd century BC

10

the suburban temple of saint venera

Not far from the Porta Giustizia (Justice Gate), the temple is situated below the modern crumbling building of the former Cirio cannery.

The ruins of the suburban temple of Saint Venera have been systematically excavated. The modern name still evokes the presence of a place dedicated to the worship of the goddess of beauty.

The archaeological evidence shows that the monumental layout of the area dates to the mid-sixth century BC although the area was certainly already inhabited in the first half of the century.

The buildings brought to light so far include a rectangular building and a large room, linked to an older structure through a monumental entrance. The portico that frames the building can be dated to a layout created in the third century BC.

A rectangular pool, whose function is uncertain and which measures 6 x 3 metres with a depth of about a metre, still preserves a baluster where a cult statue

would have been placed. The temple, which is not currently part of the itinerary for visitors to Paestum, was used until the late Imperial period. It has many Latin inscriptions and votive materials which testify to the lasting importance of the cult of Aphrodite-Venus in the area. During the early Augustan period the temple underwent significant transformations due to the generosity of several priestesses.

The beautiful statuettes of Venus come from the temple and are currently on display in the Roman section of the museum.

Statues of **Venus**
1st century BC-1st century AD

the museum of
hera argiva

The Narrative Museum of Foce Sele was created quite recently in a farmhouse dating to the 1930s in an area that used to be one of the most important and picturesque places in Magna Graecia: the temple dedicated to Hera Argiva. The museum itinerary, which uses both traditional means of display as well as video installations, multimedia products and interactive virtual reconstructions, is arranged like the plot of a story, guiding the visitor to the discovery of the temple: the journey starts from the reconstruction of the ancient landscape, and goes on to explore the illustration of the buildings of the temple, the virtual re-

construction of the monuments and the history of archaeological research, linked to two of the greatest archaeologists of our era: Umberto Zanotti Bianco and Paola Zancani Montuoro.

The heart of the museum consists of the **room of the metopes**, containing reproductions of archaic carved stone slabs which come from the temple of Hera. There are portrayals of episodes from various myths, mostly linked to the tasks of Hercules and the Trojan War. The metopes hang from the ceiling of the room and represent the visual elements of a narrative account. Using a combination of storytelling, lights and sounds, the display offers an attractive account of the myths represented in the reliefs, providing a stimulating experience for visitors.

A spiral staircase, featuring **reproductions of terracotta statuettes of the goddess**, takes visitors, accompanied by the voices and sounds of worshippers, to the lower floor where there is an

The **Narrative Museum** of Hera Argiva

Clay statuette of kneeling goddess from the Heraion of Sele 370-360 BC

Spiral staircase
with clay statuettes of Hera

observation point of the archaeological site. On the upper floor, there is a room which houses a **reconstruction of the so-called square building**. It stood near to the main temple and was probably used for weaving the *peploi* that were offered to the goddess. The temple is currently situated about 1.5 kilometres from the present coastline and about 9 kilometres from the ancient city. The geographer Strabo located the build-ing on the northern edge of Lucania and attributes the mythological foundation to Jason and the Argonauts. The temple was built in the early sixth century BC and the sacred area initially had an altar and was bounded by a portico, designed to welcome pilgrims. At the end of the sixth century BC, a large temple was built with two monumental altars in front of it. The most flourishing period in the temple's history came after the arrival of the Lucanians, at the end of the fifth century BC, with the construc-tion of new buildings that re-utilised

material from the older structures: a new portico and a meeting room situated beside it. A square building was constructed a short distance away. Numerous loom weights have been discovered which have led scholars to suggest it was where girls of marriageable age wove the *peploi* wich were offered to the goddess in an annual procession. From the second century AD, the area underwent a gradual decline until, due to the encroachment of marshes, all memory of the location of the temple slowly faded.

First floor
reconstruction of the **weaving room**

experience **paestum**

/info

visiting times and tickets
www.cilento-net.it
www.arte-m.net

park and national archaeological museum of paestum
via magna grecia 919
capaccio [sa]
www.archeosa.beniculturali. it
tel museum 0828811023

narrative museum of the temple of hera argiva
district of foce sele
masseria procuriale
via barizzo foce del sele 29
capaccio [sa]
tel 0828861440

archaeological park of velia
via contrada piana di velia
ascea marina [sa]
tel ticket office and bookshop
0974271016

for **guided tours**
and **educational workshops**
contact **le nuvole**
tel 0812395653/66
prenotazioni@arte-m.net
info@lenuvole.com

municipality of capaccio
via vittorio emanuele
tel 0828812111

for **hotels, accommodation, restaurants** and **beaches and lidos**, visit the website of the municipality of capaccio www.comune. capaccio.sa.gov.it and go to the section 'territorio', or the website of the **paestum tourist office www. infopaestum.it** and go to the section 'ospitalità'

/transport

how to get there

by car
if coming from the **north**
[rome, naples, salerno, bari]
take the a3 motorway, turn off at the **battipaglia** exit, go along the main road SS 18 heading south towards capaccio/ paestum for about 18 km, turn off at the **capaccio s.** exit and continue along via magna grecia for 5.4 km, until you come to the archaeological area
if coming from the **south**
[potenza, reggio calabria]
take the a3 motorway, turn off at the **eboli** exit, go along via san vito martire towards paestum for about 10.8 km until the **roundabout of santa cecilia**, then take the main road SS18 towards **agropoli** for about 5.5 km until the **capaccio s.** exit and continue along via magna grecia for 5.4 km, until you come to the archaeological area

by plane
capodichino airport
tel 0817896111 take the alibus from capodichino to the central railway station of naples [piazza garibaldi]; take regional or inter-regional train to sapri or paola or cosenza or reggio calabria [stops en route capaccio-roccadaspide or paestum]
salerno airport
tel 0828354311

by train
paestum station
tel 892021 without dialling a code, anywhere in Italy, only from a landline phone

/emergency and security

carabinieri station
via italia 61, 3
tel 0828725040

traffic wardens
via della repubblica 82
tel 0828723599

casualty
via borgo gromola 20
tel 0828724999

emergency medical assistance
piazza santini
tel 0828725224

many thanks to
adele campanelli, marina cipriani and all the staff of the soprintendenza who contributed to this [brief] guide and who strive every day, despite many problems, to preserve and enhance the archaeological heritage with exceptional professionalism and generosity.

select bibliography
m. cipriani, f. longo, *poseidonia e i lucani*, napoli 1996.
e. greco, f. longo, *paestum. scavi, studi, ricerche. bilancio di un decennio (1988-1998)*, paestum 2000.
g. greco, b. ferrara, *il museo narrante del santuario di hera argiva alla foce del sele*, salerno 2002.
j.g. pedley, m. torelli, *the sanctuary of santa venera at paestum I*, roma 1993.
a. pontrandolfo, a. rouveret, *le tombe dipinte a paestum*, modena 1992.
poseidonia-paestum, atti del XXVII convegno di studi sulla magna grecia (taranto 1987), napoli 1992.
p. zancani montuoro, u. zanotti bianco, *heraion I-II*, roma 1951, 1954.

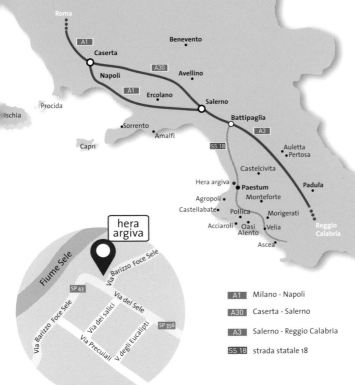

Province of Salerno

Roma

Benevento

A1

Caserta

A30

Napoli

Avellino

A1

Ercolano

Salerno

Procida

Battipaglia

Ischia

Sorrento

A3

Amalfi

Auletta
Pertosa

Capri

SS 18

Castelcivita

Hera argiva

Paestum

Padula

Agropoli

Monteforte

Castellabate

Pollica

Morigerati

Acciaroli

Velia

Reggio
Calabria

Oasi
Alento

Ascea

hera
argiva

Fiume Sele

Via Barizzo Foce Sele

SP 43

Via del Sele

Via Barizzo Foce Sele

Via dei salici

SP 356

Via Preculali

V. degli Eucalipti

A1	Milano - Napoli
A30	Caserta - Salerno
A3	Salerno - Reggio Calabria
SS 18	strada statale 18